www.finishinglinepress.com

Without a Kiss

poems by

Phoebe Nilsen

Finishing Line Press
Georgetown, Kentucky

Without a Kiss

ACKNOWLEDGMENTS

I would like to thank my husband, Viktor, for his unwavering faith, his
encouragement and his steadfast, loving support.

Publisher: Leah Maines
Editor: Christen Kincaid
Cover Art: Ambrogio Bellotti
Author Photo: Viktor Nilsen
Cover Design: Elizabeth Maines McCleavy

Printed in the USA on acid-free paper.
Order online: www.finishinglinepress.com
                also available on amazon.com

Author inquiries and mail orders:
Finishing Line Press
P. O. Box 1626
Georgetown, Kentucky 40324
U. S. A.

Table of Contents

"O, how this spring of love resembleth
The uncertain glory of an April day,
Which now shows all the beauty of the sun,
And by and by a cloud takes all away!"

William Shakespeare, *The Two Gentlemen of Verona*

The Gondola

She stopped dusting,
took the cheap souvenir off the shelf
where it had stood for years,
cradled it in her palm
as if it were alive,
and once again heard his voice,
young as it was then,

"Are you dating?"

He had caught her off guard,
getting off one night train
to board another,
and having never dated,
she hesitated. But
without waiting for an answer,
he had quipped,

"I don't know about you,
but I am."

So this was dating. She had thought
they were just travelling
on a current of joy,
enough to last a lifetime.

They were too poor to hire
a gondola that night, yet more
exuberant in their innocence
than they would be the
rest of their lives.

"Why are you smiling, Mom?"

"Oh, nothing," she replied, replacing the
souvenir of *life* on its shelf,
the place now nearly forgotten.

The Train

I see us there, running,
dust flying,
almost bumping into women
shopping at fruit stands,
children flying kites,
lovers out for a stroll, and us
running, still running to catch the last train.

There's no money for hotels,
and school starts in less than a day.

We're panting heavily,
but the train is unaware
and will not wait.

I check the impulse to
grab your arm or hand
to summon strength
for the last stretch,
the station within sight.

We make it, and gasping
recover the life
that seemed exhaled.

Years later I learn
you checked yourself too that day,
and in each other's eyes we
glimpse what has expired,
in the distance, the terminal and
the tail end of our train.

Destinations

Past midnight
on a deserted train in Venice
waiting for dawn
and the train to move us
toward our destination,
you sat across from me, but
only for a minute,
then asked to rest your head on my lap,
moved over,
and in the dark
I must have seemed almost
beautiful to you.

Reaching up, you
removed my glasses and
seeing me naked then
for the first time,
praised the arch of my brows.

Who knows what else you were thinking or
hoped to undress when
you inquired if I was cold,
took the hand I held against my chest,
the other being under your head but
with my cape between.

The appropriate second or two and I
withdrew my hand, as you
loosened your grip, reluctantly?

Too late to undo the move,
I saw my own desire in your pretext,
cursed myself then and
a thousand times since,
knowing how different our journey might have been,
had I just let my hand linger.

Heritage Canyons

Cascading Colorado desire,
turbulent and white
flimsy veils,
containing, cutting
canyons too grand
for its flood to reach
parched shores.

Crystal as the azure pools I dream of,
close as the head on my lap,
yet as far from easing
thirst on its banks
as your lips from quenching mine.

And the walls of my heritage remain
while the freedom of yours rushes by
ancient stones
sparkling in transparent view,

unaware of the conquest
that might have been yours,
had you seen your reflection in my eyes.

Divided

After Venice, Florence and Pisa,
we sat side by side on a suitcase
in a crowded aisle, penniless
but peerless, forgetting
Creation ended, perfection
only for a week.

"Come on," I teased,
"You sing, I'll
collect the money!"

It was no paradise, yet
our souls were one
back then,
though we lacked the guts to
let our bodies follow.

It seems too, you feared
my color would
rub off on you,
wall out your goals.

Those were different times.

No matter, the walls rose higher, higher.
Our Jericho was not about to fall.

Still, I left myself open,
waiting for your body…
received
endless echoes,
the distant percussion of a train
against your failing serenade,

"Buona sera signorina,
kiss me goodnight,"
and the lips unable to follow.

Boboli Gardens

How could we, so young
and captivated, walk together
in these Florentine gardens
with statues, fountains, hidden
tree-lined walkways for lovers,
spring sun warm on our cheeks,
still resist what every nerve in our
starving bodies begged for,
refrain from holding hands or
walking arm in arm at least?

What monstrous law or fear
prevented us? What shame, shyness or
risk great enough to paralyze the healthy,
leaving eyes and voices free to play?

A scream wants out.
What was wrong with us?

Now in the far north and out at sea,
seagulls hover and squawk overhead
begging fishermen for scraps.

The sea withholds its gifts today.
Their cries in vain,
nothing happens.
Nobody bothers to listen.

Some days the sea yields sustenance,
other days nothing. That's just how it is.

Easter in Florence

Only once he put his arm around her,
helped her across a chaotic street
she wished were three miles wide
and later led another down the bridal aisle
of the candlelit renaissance church
whose frescoes and statues they had admired.

Yet if transported there again
neither could ever name the street
or find the church
that could not capture the moment,
immortalize in its arches
the burning mold of an uncertain, trembling hand
on a girl's back,
sculpting its secret sanctuary,
casting what she could not prolong
in its pillar lined aisles,
marking a crossroad,
inscribing and sealing a stone
that would never be rolled away.

Love's Cathedral

She came to you there
without one plea,
and still you would not join her song.

Truth is,
you knew it would be flawed,
for she is not a singer.

Unrivalled
you strive for that perfect score,
success and honor your rewards,

while she just lives,

and her poor song
rises alone.

Mysteriously glorified
it echoes in each crevice,

marred only by
your silence.

Pisa Revisited

Today I stood on the soil
from which my heart was made,
the love of life first planted by your gaze
and might have grown into a cypress but
for lack of rain.

Instead there is a leaning tower there,
tall, defiantly crafted and admired,
while in its hidden vaults
our grace starved youth lies buried.

Buried

Where I grew up girls waited,
were taught, expected to wait,
queens, Nefertitis awaiting excavation.

So I waited
until you came and resurrected me,
but only briefly,
as if to say, "This is the life you can have.
Now go get it."

But what you're taught from birth
is not so easily discarded. I kept on waiting.
This time I knew it was for you.

You are a grandfather now,
and I'm no longer waiting.

But you remain in the casket within, and there
it still feels like waiting. There
you are always seventeen, King Tut.
Isn't that also how you still feel inside?
No receding hairline and wrinkle free,
distant as the year we met but

clear as the butterfly close to my hand,
the child's boat upon a wave,
the evening star,
still beckoning, always out of reach,

just as you were
when you sat across from me, and your eyes
said we were one,

on a train to different destinations.

Approaching the terminal now, I wonder,
will future generations unearth your golden casket
when they come digging for the silent past in me?

Nocturnal Archaeologist

Unexpected midnight visitor
prepared for a dig in forbidden ground,
expectantly held what you will never hold,
with pope-like reverence
embraced, bent
and lips wet
unkissed earth
dissolving
decades of dignity and reserve,
while Samson and Goliath wrestled within us,
struggling nobly, rent the mummy gauze veil,
exposed the mask, stood awed
at its preserved condition
in the forgotten desert
eyes resisting
fear in mine,
revealing what gods ordained buried
by century vows,
prying open sleep-locked lids
that dared unveil
and look upon
that ancient, sacred
love shroud.

Casually

I approach slowly,
wondering whether you'd arrived already,
hoping you hadn't,
hoping you'd see me first,
be the one to draw near,
recognize, confirm,
take the first step.

But there's a crowd already, and you—
as always—in the center.

Then for once, the crowd parts
as I move closer
and simultaneously we stand
with arms outstretched.
We hug, let go,
hold at arm's length,
look each other in the eye and
hug again.

Later I think what we both
would have given for that hug
thirty years ago. But now we
take it in stride and talk

casually

about our work, our travels, our children.

That night
I weep for the young girl
who never held your hand
though she cradled you
for years
in her dreams.

Reunion Bridge

Fumbling whirlpools
under evaporated years
a bridge now burnt

and two

forever on different banks
knowing water will not rush backwards
and the bridge will not be built by their hands

unaware of
silent beaver years
damming the wild river
into a quiet pool where

silver now,
they salmon to love's birthplace

and watch
departed whitewater struggles
return rainbow refractions
to imprisoned eyes

lighting that constant
invisible arch
without a touch.

Sorry

"I'm sorry I hurt you," you said decades later
and seemed to mean it too.

"You didn't," I said. No elaborations then.

I did not say how I had loved you for months,
longing for but not expecting you to notice,
knowing I was unnoticeable, always the admirer
not the admired.

I did not say I was overjoyed when I thought
my luck had turned, when you noticed,
called it an honor that I accepted your invitation.

I did not say you delighted me
in ways I had until then only imagined,

though there was no touch,
no kiss,
no embrace

when just as unexpectedly you withdrew, vanished.

Your desire had ebbed,
I had been too serious, too reserved,
or your feelings too overpowering,
unknown territory then,
greater than both of us.

We were so young.

Most of all, I did not say I know you
kissed my hair ever so lightly,
only when you thought I had fallen asleep,
my head on your shoulder.

Why do you think you hurt me?
Did you know it then?
Know that your smiles, your voice, your looks
gave promises you did not dare endorse
with words, with a clasp of your hand on mine,
with a single kiss?

Know that you denied your own heart,
withheld life?

There was no quarrel, no betrayal with another,
no anger or hate,
nothing but what was left unsaid.

You only planted the seed that
might have flourished, borne fruit.

How could you have known?
It was all inside me.

Though perhaps you see it,
feel the pain now
when even the hope of resurrection
is beyond reach.

Three Missing Words

They talked with ease in an early mist
of admiration, challenge, respect
no topic barred
existentialism to marriage to sex

and rising dawn's ambitious hues
flamed unseen
surged to please
and be found worthy of the scrutinous day

while tantalizing evening's eye-locking veil
intensified 'chance' meetings
under campus lights
on dormitory steps
in cafeteria foyers
student lounges
and library halls

talking
listening
talking

until all was said

but those mutually longed for
deeply anchored
tied
knotted
fettered
chained
locked in solitary confinement words

that cut their nights apart.

A Snake Would Strip

Skin me with distant laser eyes
but don't deny love-taught desire
smiling to smithereens a maiden's head
scarring your name in bleeding flesh
initialing a life for you unfurled
first sought then spurned

Peel this tan parched onion film
and let my burning tears
cleanse your blurred sight

A snake would strip
lust undressing hunger
shed the offensive color at your feet,
while innocence trapped in silent jaws
dumbly wondered
seeing angelic slyness' bridegroom
whitely bedded

yet now a still starving stricken
servile soul squirms
as skilled scalpel looks
confidently lift
love's hidden cataract
exposing
apple of the eye
color blinded vision.

Lazarus Dreams

Unheard, unseen, unmoving,
her dry lips cried
your champagne name
ship just departed
drowning in dry tears

and closed eyes watched you vanish
cyclone train doors closing.

Prevented by security vow guards,
she collapsed when you handed your boarding pass.

A quarter century removed,
her cry still echoes,
mercilessly explodes,
burning your workaholic days,

and in your parched dreams,
untasted wine spilled,
you drink to her only
with Lazarus eyes
longing to hush that silence
echoing and exploding
in your chest.

Base Fear

He led her to the base of Mount Olives,
hunger mirrored in stones like loaves
yet to be dipped in blood, sweat, tears,
and struggling, chose to say goodbye,
however tenderly, gripped by desire,
fearing ascension,
or a momentary transfiguration
in a shared death-moment panoramic review
of a glorious inheritance,
a glimpse of what they might have had.

At the peak
she looks down
and sees a miniature man retreating,
smugly adjusting his victory halo.

But she had never been a temptress
caught in sin.

Arrivederci

He was taken aback. But why?
He knew she was right, and he
no correspondent.

Just the same.
It was only politeness.
She could have given him that.

Yet he felt soaked in guilt,
not knowing why:

for dropping her so easily
without a word because
all promises had been wordless,
for not holding her when he could have,
for fearing her closeness now,
or for still wanting her so much.

And so, you could hardly call it a hug
when very lightly, almost
gingerly, he touched her shoulders,
leaning in, still ensuring
plenty of space between them, but

he was close enough to smell her hair, and
closer than he had ever been when
they were free to hold.

"We'll keep in touch," he said,
and she, "I don't think so."

It was too late for that, though
she did not say so.

The Atheist

I keep waiting for a letter I'm
almost sure will never come.

Still, I wait.

I'm ninety-nine percent atheist, but then
there's that sliver of a percent,
ever present chance
there's something out there
beyond the stars, that created
the stars, that created me
and planted

that one percent seed that

you are still alive, and I
am still alive in you
out there somewhere,

so that even if
you never send that letter,
the proof I'm waiting for,
the proof you still care, remember though
that dimension we never asked for, time,
has come between,

that love grain refuses to die,
still begs to live in your
invisible presence.

Smiles

My body is heavy with
accumulated years tonight.
It sags to the ground.

Then out of nowhere
I see your gap-toothed smile,
and I am seventeen again.

The aches and longings are unchanged, but I
have grown free and more eloquent now.

Our conversations would surprise you
if you could participate.

Love does not die, you say,
no matter how deeply we
are forced to bury it. It grows
and surfaces in mysterious smiles
while life lasts, and blooms
each spring hereafter
in the unstoppable lilies
forcing their way
through the rich soil
of our valleys.

Curtain Fall

My eyes are shut
against tubes, blinking monitors, doctors in white coats.
They think I am too drugged to hear or
comprehend the diagnosis though
the terms are clear and leave no room for doubt.

Unseen the curtain falls black
in my face
as it did so long ago, the day I learned
you had signed away your young life
until death. Your choice, and I so very
unprepared. Dazed, I wept, grieved, mourned
for years. Death seemed so far away.
Life would be long without my dearest friend.

It was long. Much longer than you grasped, I bet,
when you said, "I do."

But now the end is near I hear them say,
and no tears trickle at this dark curtain fall.
The news, a simple detail. There is no choice,
no alternative, no other way. It is not
unexpected.

Only briefly now, the curtain lifts again.
I smile, my ultimate bow to fate.
"There is no parting there," I whisper
with my last breath, "nothing more to take."

Then silently, so silently, the final curtain falls.
I slip away unnoticed.
Only cool darkness remains.

Phoebe Nilsen (née Watson) was born in Cairo, Egypt in 1949. Her family moved to Oshawa, Ontario, the summer she turned fifteen. The move from a traditional and very conservative Egyptian environment to the unaccustomed freedom of the West had a marked impact on her life. The conflicts and difficulties encountered in learning to adjust to a new world of flirting and dating became the driving force behind her poetry.

After completing the first two years of college in Oshawa, she spent a year studying German in Austria. Following that, she completed her BA with a double major in English and German at Columbia Union College, Maryland, and in 1970, her MA in English at Andrews University, Michigan. She subsequently taught high school and college in many places, including Nevada, Iowa; Walla Walla, Washington; Benton Harbor, and Berrien Springs, Michigan; and Toronto, Ontario.

In 1973-74 she took a year off from teaching to go to Tromsø, Norway, where she met her husband. They got married in Canada in 1976 and later lived in Michigan, Ontario, and Saskatchewan before moving back to Norway in 1984. After dedicating thirteen years to raising their four children, Phoebe returned to teaching in 1990. She taught in Glomfjord, Bodø and Levanger, Norway. Finally, she spent the last twenty-one years of her career at Nord-Trøndelag University College (now Nord University), near Trondheim, Norway, where she was associate professor. She taught ESL methodology and English literature to Norwegian teacher trainees and held numerous in-service courses for Norwegian English teachers. She was also involved in many international educational projects and enjoyed traveling to many countries in Europe and to the US. She also spent six weeks working at a research institute near Shanghai, China, an assignment facilitated by the Norwegian Research Foundation. She retired in 2012 and now enjoys travelling, writing poetry when the mood strikes and spending time with her five grandchildren.